WORD MOVIES

FRUSTRATED BIRD

if you think it's okay
for the first day of May
then don't go away, go away
frustrated bird
singin' in the unexpected snow
no one told you
no one clued you in
about the weather in my yard
I guess they just expected
that you'd know

but just wait
it's not too late
soon it will change
it always does
frustrated bird, don't go
don't quit singing
in the unexpected snow

soon the sun will shine prettily
in your immediate vicinity
and all this corruption will go
frustrated bird don't go
don't quit singing
in the unexpected snow

if you think it's okay
for the first day of May
then don't go away go away
frustrated bird don't go

WORD MOVIES
BY JOHN HARTFORD

DOUBLEDAY & COMPANY, INC. GARDEN CITY, NEW YORK
1971

Designed by Earl Tidwell

Library of Congress Catalog Card Number 72-138933

Oh the world goes on
in the key of D
around my head
in harmony.
In simple thirds
it plays for me
in its tonic,
subdominant and
major keys—

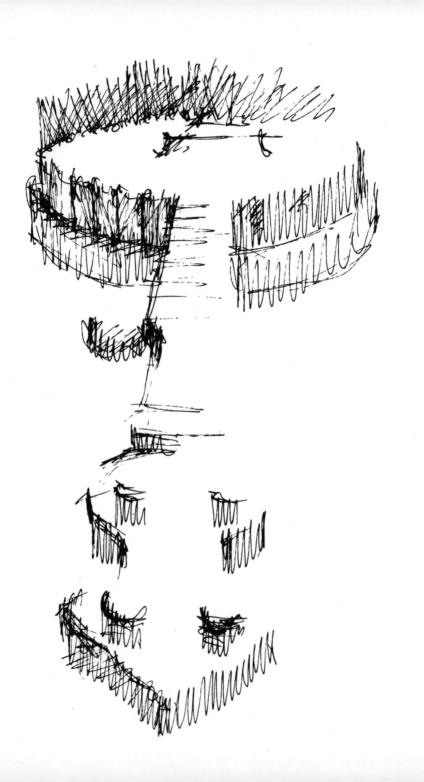

don't quit singing
in the unexpected snow

frustrated bird don't go
don't quit singing
in the unexpected snow

NAKED IN SPITE OF MYSELF

this tongue of yours
so razor sharp
has cut me deep within
I feel as though
your fingernails
had stripped me
of my skin
and could not bear
to hear your voice
or feel your icy touch
I'm one outside
alone I find
I'm naked
in spite of myself

my brain is burning up inside
my eyes go fiery red
my pride has turned to ashes now
right here
inside my head
my fingers slip in silence
from the things I dearly held
I'm one outside
alone I find
I'm naked
in spite of myself

I'm guilty here
with no excuse
I cannot say I tried
no place to turn
no place to run
no hole where I can hide
no hope of walking out to find
some other kind of hell
I'm one outside
alone I find
I'm naked
in spite of myself

my feet are numb
on broken glass
as on this spot I stand
I only asked for mercy
but you spat into my hand
the words that split my eardrums now
drown out all pleas for help
I'm one outside
alone I find
I'm naked
in spite of myself

OPEN ROAD ODE

I'd like to get back
on the open road
as far as the eye
can see
for the open road
is a good woman's love
and somewhere I know
that it's waiting for me

a street is like a
stranger to me
an alley can be
like a friend
a boulevard
like a noisy old drunk
on a sidewalk
that has no end

I used to ride
your black top slab
we used to travel alone
you used to be
the open road
but now all I see
is a no parking zone

I'd like to get back
on the open road
as far as the eye
can see
for the open road
is a good woman's love
and somewhere I know
that it's waiting for me

FRONT PORCH

my front porch looks right at the back
porch
at the side of your house sits my car
your laundry hangs there by my window
in the sun that shines down in our yard

when I come home I see you a leavin'
when I'm leavin' you're just pullin' in
at times I could reach out and touch you
but I'm not even sure of your name

I saw you last round about midnight
from the front porch you seemed so
carefree
like you never could ever be happy
to live in the country with me

I came up here huntin' for riches
or fortune and fame I had heard
but too long I've stared at your back
porch
and now I'm a slave to your world

when the hair on my head turns to silver
my feet and my hands old and sore
I'll prop my old chair on the front porch
and gaze at your old kitchen door

TO SAY

to say
that I've stopped changing
is to say
that I've stopped growing
and to say
that I've stopped growing
is to admit
that I am dead

oh when my body stops
and my brain has to
slam on its brakes
will it skid on
a few more feet
before it crashes

to say
that I'm a thinker
is to say
that I know something
and to say
that I know something
is nothing
in itself

oh when my poetry stops
and my mouth has to
slam on its brakes
will it skid on
a few more feet
before it whispers

to say
that I'm imperfect
is to say
that I am human
and to say
that I am human
is perfection
in itself

oh when my body stops
and my brain has to
slam on its brakes
will it skid on
a few more feet
before it crashes

I'VE GOT A MIND TO MOVE ON

you take the past
and stay on the farm
live where you've lived
since the day you were born
I'll take a chance
on the things that may come
I'll travel the highway
My face to the sun
I've got a mind
to move on

you take the fields
and the hot dusty rows
live with it, die with it
I've got to go
and draw me a bead
on a far mountain crest
I'll throw my luck
to the wind and the west
I've got a mind
to move on

I'll never be satisfied
this I know well
someday when you see me
I'll bid you farewell
my clothes on my back
my feet headed west
I'll turn my back
on the land you love best
I've got a mind
to move on

WHEN MOTHER NATURE CALLS HER WAYWARD SON

when nature calls
her wayward son
with leather finger
crooked and narrow
beckons a voice
a wind of sorrow come
that I be torn
to go or stay
that you might then
with no assurance
I return
might rise and drift away
the ponies stand
in muted rows
in flattened music
weaving in the autumn sun
a child in liberation runs
down through the
paisley colored halls
where echoes mother nature's call
I tend the ancient purple sore
that rends my heart
in peeling walls
that tears apart
like some forgotten door
then running on my knees
must fall
to kiss your hand
and have it all
when mother nature calls

NATURAL TO BE GONE

you don't know me
where I live
my tracks may soon
go everywhere
because there ain't
no other place
for them to go
where I'm from
outside of now
for me that's really
hard to say
like sometimes
I'm not really
sure I even
know

what's the difference
being different
when it's difference now
that looks alike
you say I'm changing
I'm not sure that's wrong
it's just the center line
on this highway
runs up my banjo neck
and I feel
somehow
that it's natural
to be gone

what crazy patterns
do we follow
sitting knee to knee

upon some river bank somewhere
at supper time
the evening air is moving
like molasses
towards the sticky night
so easy
as I press your hand in mine

what's the difference
being different
when it's difference
now that looks alike
you say I'm changing
I'm not sure that's wrong
today it may be natural
sitting here discussing it
tomorrow
just as natural
to be gone

there's no season
in my mind
that I can count on
for an answer
and I've dug too many holes
expecting snow
I'm not sure
to where I'm headed
how I'll ride
and who I'm with
if I return
or when I think
that I might go
you seem
a little colder
when I say
I must be leaving
what an ugly way for us
to let it end

what's the use
in being worried
cause I'm going in an hour
when the time
is running out
that we can spend

what's the difference
being different
when it's difference now
that looks alike
you say I'm changing
I'm not sure that's wrong
today it may be natural
sitting here discussing it
tomorrow
just as natural
to be gone

LIFE PRAYER

I love life
every morning I wake up
saying in the back of my mind
this could be my last day on earth
this could be the last time I'll ever feel the wind
raising the hair on my body
or the touch of my feet to the ground
or the warmth of your flesh next to mine
this could be the last chance I'll have
to watch all kinds of people
doing all kinds of things
and thinking all kinds of thoughts
in all kinds of directions around me
this might be my last chance
to spend everything I've saved
since last night
or hear all your sounds ringing through my head
it might even be my last chance
to be sick
I'm like a child
trying to do everything
say everything
see everything
and be everything
all at once
should I wake up some morning
God help me
and find myself bored
among the walking dead

I WOULD NOT BE HERE

I would not be here
If I hadn't been there
I wouldn't been there
if I hadn't just turned
on Wednesday the third
in the late afternoon
got to talking with George
who works out in the back
and only because
he was getting off early
to go see a man
at a Baker Street bookstore
with a rare first edition
of steamboats and cotton
a book he would never
have sought in the first place
had he not been inspired
by a fifth grade replacement
school teacher in Kirkwood
who was picked just at random
by some man on a school board
who couldn't care less
and she wouldn't been working
if not for her husband
who moved two months prior
to work in the office
of a man he had met
while he served in the army
and only because
they were in the same barracks

an accident caused
by a poorly made roster
mixed up on the desk
of a sergeant from Denver
who wouldn't be in
but for being in back
in a car he was riding
before he enlisted
that hit a cement truck
and killed both his buddies
but a back seat flew up there
and spared him from dying
and only because
of the fault of a workman
who forgot to turn screws
on a line up in Detroit
'cause he hollered at Sam
who was hateful that morning
hung over from drinking
alone at a tavern
because of a woman
he wished he'd not married
he met long ago
at a Jewish bar mitzvah
for the son of a man
who had moved there from Jersey
who managed the drugstore
that sold the prescription
that cured up the illness
he caught way last summer
he wouldn't have caught
except . . .

THEM GOOD OLD BOYS

here's to all them
good old boys
cheer 'em on
and make a
lot of noise
for this world
would be a
bad old place
without a lot of
good old boys

A SIMPLE THING AS LOVE

when you come across unto me
with your hair the tangled grass
of evening breezes
and you do not hide your face
because somebody said one time
it wasn't natural
what a joy for us just running
down this crooked trail of midnight
and the peaceful things inside me
that it does
then you whisper low I have to go
the acid tears start coming slow
to complicate a simple thing
as love

awake now I don't hear the floor boards
creaking
as you walk
back from the window
or feel your satin fingers
drawing patterns on my back
where I lay dying
without you I'm a child
who sucks the vacant thumb of
emptiness
left crying
when he has not had enough
at the mercy of an empty room
sing verses to some faded wall
confused about a simple thing
as love

it's too bad we couldn't stay here
till the clock runs out and falls
from sheer exhaustion
or till morning when I watch you
as you stoop
to pick your things
up from the floor
but too soon for us it's over
in the shock of the electric light bulb
sunrise
in the ceiling up above
as it dangles to remind us
of the spiderweb that binds us
and just complicates a simple thing
as love

MEANWHILE YOU SIT BY MY BANJO

wouldn't it be incredible
as I write my weary song
that you could be
beside me there
inside my head
to see what takes so long
wouldn't it be incredible
you could sit and hold my hand
and you could hear
the same things
I am listening for
I know it must be boring
to be with me by yourself
while I'm up here
all sprawled out
at the table
and all you have
are promises
of far out things to come
the best
that I can give you
while I'm able

but meanwhile you sit
by my banjo alone
with your hair hangin' down
by your side
the night might be long
while you wait by my banjo
I'm letting my thoughts
get me high

the room is growing quieter
but somewhere I can hear
a circus of cathedral bells
a ringing
your eyelids must be heavy
as the hour passes slow
but I must get it down
while it is singing

I'm writing just as quickly
as I make my fingers move
so I can get it down
where I can read it
and then in just a little while
I'll do it right out loud
the only way
that I can share it with you

TODAY

lost forever
is yesterday
and I don't believe
in tomorrow
I used to dream
of a pot of gold
and it
only
brought me
sorrow
I used to think
that the road stretched on
till it went
this whole world
round
but now I've learned
to live my life
before
the sun
goes down

for tomorrow
when it finally
comes
and the curtain of dawn
fades away
the hopes
of many
are crushed
to dust
when they find
it ain't nothing
but today

27

and every day
I grow and die
as tho
it might be my last
and kiss the minute
what a thankful smile
and turn my back
on the past
and wink
at tomorrow
it don't scare me
I only live
in today
while you
might sit
with your fingers crossed
and watch it all fade away

for tomorrow
when it finally
comes
and the curtain of dawn
fades away
the hopes
of many
are crushed
to dust
when they find
it ain't nothing
but today

LANDSCAPE GROWN COLD

the trees standing naked
the ground underfoot
is a dark cellar cool
the battleship sky
is so heavy
my shoulders droop
it's a lean kind of day
that I sometimes pass through

the vines are like veins
on the old village wall
where the grass turns to white
and way down the road
I see smoke from another world
removed from my life

I sit in the ditch
and I dig in the sand
with the heel of my soul
sink down
in my coat collar back
to the wind that blows
insane by myself
in a landscape grown cold

the painted tin sign
flaps back in the wind
where the green bottles lay
and a window of boards
facing hollow
upon the dust

empty the chairs
sit in judgment
accusing the day

I sit in the ditch
and I dig in the sand
with the heel of my soul
sink down
in my coat collar back
to the wind that blows
insane by myself
in a landscape grown cold

EARTHWORDS

as I stand here
breathing
thigh deep
in the weeds of ignorance
that cover the breast
of the earth
don't let the blue laws
of communication
keep the fresh air
out of the rooms of my mind
or extinguish the sun
in my belly
and don't let my hallways
and stairwells become empty
except for my pitifully
huddled form
crying
in some dark musty corner
in defeat
because someone
forgot to tell me long ago
that there's nothing dirty
about earth

all I ask is
to squat here in the cool shade
and talk to you
forgetting the games and rules
ingrained in the fiber
of my personality
and let me not be worried
about what I look like
or sound like to you

and let me breathe
easy and feel natural
and not get confused
or hung up
trying to express earth feeling
without earth words
and please don't get hysterical
to the point
that you would
cut out my tongue
just because I said I loved you
or scratch out my eyes
because in all your ugliness
I said
you were beautiful

just bear with me
and if you feel
some small part
of what I have to say
and if ever the day should come
that we're in a position
to study each other's faces
let me understand
that you feel what I've had to say
not because
you thought you were supposed to feel it
but because you really did

this white page is really black except
for the white areas
acknowledging these words
and the black is really white
except for the black areas
that define the white . . .
the black and white so depend on each other
Sound cannot be sound
unless it is acknowledged by silence
the "is" and the "isn't"

so depend on each other
A soul doesn't really feel it is a soul
until some other soul
acknowledges awareness of its presence . . .
people so depend on each other
Escaping from indifference
and possessed of a basic natural showmanship
we each try to prove we exist
during our short journey to the grave . . .
searching for love and hate . . .
that we may confront them and hear them say
either "you is" or
"you ain't" . . . then at least we know
"we are"

Loneliness can be a wonderful thing
it can turn you on with the beautifully
terrifying confusion of things
as your sense of alone expands
into itself . . . and then explodes
reeling in cartwheels
through endless skyways of the mind
but
loneliness
in all its loneliness
cannot exist by itself

I never did say I was from anywhere
'less it was just from my mommy's tummy
and I never did say I was goin' anywhere
'less it was just over yonder
but then someday I'll wind up in the
tummy of mommy earth

In my meandering I sometimes wonder
what it would be like to peel off
all this chrome veneer of society
unhand everybody and EVERYBODY
stand around in their old bones and stringy

muscle fibers and see
if we can find out what "understanding"
really is . . .
millions of extras in some gigantic movie
where there are no stars . . . or
elements in some huge joke
where laughter is secondary only to love
but
did anybody hear the punch line?

the more you scratch
the more you itch
and
the more you itch
the more you scratch
some people scratch their arms
with needles
and their throats with pills
their eyeballs with colors
their eardrums with tones
and we all scratch love
(or hate)
in one way or another
I scratch banjo strings
(among other things)
and pieces of paper
with an old stub of a pencil
and
the more I scratch
the more it itches

SQUAT

squat by the car
by the tree
by old boards
by old nails
squat by the
back stoop
in the shade
in the grass
and carve twigs
squat by the road
and draw lines in the dust
in the sand
in the yellow white sun
squat by the
post office
in the cool shadow
spit and talk
and spit and talk some more
squat at the end of the row
squat and drink
squat and pull
small dead leaves
drink mop and rise
to squat no more
squat by the pit and spit
and bet and cuss
and watch and
grin some more
squat down
when there's no reason
to stand or lean
do not sit or lie down
but like the others
squat down

DAYTIME OF LIFE

awake in the dawn
of the cold misty dewlight
kicking and drinking
warm milk while I'm crying
in the sterilized smell
of my unsure surroundings
feeling warm hands
as I'm passed back and forth
and I'm
wiggling and crawling
and reaching out slowly
strange sounds
at my elbow
but no way to make them
the shapes of big colors
and lights
all around me
comin' to grips
with the cold hard linoleum
pushing and pulling
as I travel in circles
unsure on my knees
as I crawl
towards the table
unsteady on legs
as I'm finding my balance
my legs
stretching out
and a wish
to go walking
out in the road
in the gravel and sunshine
out on the earth

with my feet
in the short grass
the shadows
of barn and garage
learning quickly
a switch
to my bottom
and on the bed
crying
in the dawn
of the morning
the vague early morning
at the start
of the daytime of life

standing out here
by an old pile of lumber
a long shiny track
that's still silently ringing
from the last southbound freight
that was two o'clock passing
and I in my levis
my cigarettes
twisted
in the arm of a t shirt
I'm smart
like a rooster
you stand here
in front of me
heavily breathing
your long brown hair
matted with sweat
as we're silent
the beads
like last Christmas
that lay
on your bosom
I feel
the exploding of

some
innerself
that's
more lasting
and longing
than the carcass surrounding
the bursting of love
that is pleading now
for you
that creeps
in our eyes
and it colors our thinking
and tingles our hands
and our arms
and our foreheads
as the flesh is now talking
in words that are quiet
in the hot afternoon
as we're making our plans
as we walk
through the daytime
of life
a baby comes crying
and laughing
and kicking
and drinking
warm milk
as it's handled
so gently
and afternoon
comes
to see three
other babies
playing
and running
their bodies
fast growing
sundown comes sneaking
around

by the back door
my joints getting stiffer
and moving
more slowly
my hair getting thinner
and turning
to driftwood
then going down hill
in the still
of the evening
so peaceful and gentle
I'm not
in a hurry
just passing the grave
of a friend
I once
played with
the pine needles soft
underfoot
as I'm walking
and children come running
to guide their
grandfather
and if you dont mind
I'll just
sit in
the shadows
and rest and go slowly
I'm getting so
tired
my head on a pillow
a doctor now holding
my wrist as he's feeling
the veins barely throbbing
my grandchildren standing
around by my bedside
and now through the mist

I can faint see them crying
but I will be comfortable
here on the cushions of silk
all around me
I think
I must sleep
in the cool
deep
and it's midnight

BAKING SODA

hooray for bakin' soda
ain't it neat
and cheers for
national bakin' soda week
for folks that's young
and folks that's old
bicarbonate of soda
will cure that cold
it cleans your teeth
and prevents the flu
and you can use it
in your car battery too
it puts out fires
of fat or grease
pass the bakin' soda
please
now
if your biscuits
cakes or pies
absolutely refuse
to rise
get the stuff
that's always slick
that bakin' soda
does the trick
and if you're feeling
far from placid
from an over excess
of stomach acid
just step right up and yell
don't stammer
get a big mess

of that arm and hammer
and if you cannot
clean your dentures
with any other
commercial ventures
from Portland Maine
to North Dakota
smart folks dunk
in bakin' soda
but beware your fun you botch
this ain't the kind
you mix with scotch

THE COLLECTOR

he slips in around you
when you are asleep
through attics and closets
he silently creeps
a small piece of cardboard
a bottlecap there
an old ball of string
or a long strand of hair
a match from the kitchen
the tooth of a comb
with barely a sound
he turns and goes home

the collector is waiting
to look through your trash
to handle your beads
and pull at your sash
to read through your papers
and look in your room
then gently withdraw
to his own kind of gloom
and then with a sigh
and nothing to say
the collector goes quietly
squeaking away

your thimbles are missing
the hammer is gone
and the light in the basement
it shouldn't be on
he sniffs at your flowers
and takes an old shoe
and goes through your scrapbook

before he is through
examines your figures
your cards and your dates
and then the collector
just evaporates

he slips in around you
when you are asleep
through attics and closets
he silently creeps
a small piece of cardboard
a bottlecap there
an old ball of string
or a long strand of hair
a match from the kitchen
the tooth of a comb
with barely a sound
he turns and goes home

UNTANGLE YOUR MIND

you're stretchin' and strainin'
and bendin' too hard
till all of the chickens
have run from your yard
alone in the doorway
a gun in your hand
you'd better untangle
your mind

you try not to listen
to the children upstairs
who laugh at you nervously
sitting down there
the shiny blue metal
lies cold in your lap
you'd better untangle
your mind

you worry the morning
you worry the night
you worry for something
that's not yet in sight
your worry is rotten
your head is on fire
you'd better untangle
your mind

your engine is whinin'
you're sunk in the mud
your wheels only spin
and you can't see the hub
your face hangin' back
you have covered your eyes
and you'd better untangle
your mind

relax or youll snap
like a string in a strain
without your umbrella
go out in the rain
just look in the treetops
and let it come down
and try and untangle
your mind

don't think of tomorrow
or even next hour
taste only the sweet things
forget all the sour
it's getting too heavy
to set in this chair
without you untangle
your mind

THE CATEGORY STOMP

now you
put your right foot
on the left
and you
bring your left foot
down
with your
hands in your pocket
and your
chin up high
you turn about
halfway around
don't do
the double shuffle
or the
jackson drag
'cause you
might be a dancin'
in an unhip bag
it's
the
folk country
discotecing
soft rock
contemporary
abstract
expressionism
word movie
flower power
hard raga
neo blue grass
stone billy

dirty boogie
freaked out
and comin' on
and jelly bean
and
psychedelic stomp

now you
spread your knees
and dance on your toes
cross your fingers
on the end of your nose
drag your elbows
down on the floor
then you turn a somersault
and do it once more
then it's
back in the middle
with a do si do
but a little more sigh
and a little less do
now down on your belly
with your knees up tight
and roll out the door
till you're plumb
out of sight

LOVE IS SWEETER

it's easier to loaf
on a busy day
when there's lots of work
to be done
I can drink more water
when it's hot and dry
and my throat has been
scorched
by the sun
you feel pretty small
when you study the sky
as far as the eye can see
and love is sweeter
when you're all alone
the way that
you left me

the shadows turn black
in the middle of the day
when the sun is high
in the sky
and lights get brighter
in the middle of the night
where there wasn't any light
to see by
I pass not the place
where we sat yesterday
where you rested your head
on my knee
and love is sweeter
when you're all alone
the way that
you left me

GO FALL ASLEEP NOW

tomorrow takes its toll on me
but what care I if it should be
last cigarette and cup of tea
and by the night no longer see your face
I fall asleep now

and when the blinding sun comes by
the night man heaves his weary sigh
the railroad whistle's mournful cry
will call to me but now I try to rest
and fall asleep now

the papers blow in silence down
the empty streets of dusty towns
there is no traffic comin' down
to stop at green lights turning now to red
go fall asleep now

my tired body rolls its way
down underneath the bedclothes stay
pretending it can't move this way
escaping from the coming day go try
and fall asleep now

don't think about the distant morn
when once again the world is born
and from your side I must be torn
so curl up close I'll keep you warm
come here and go to sleep now

THE TALL TALL GRASS

now August is a wicked month
a pleasure yet so bad
escape from all the hopes and fears
a time to laugh a time for tears
and run away from the rest of the year
and love in the tall tall grass

the August sun's a wicked sun
it tans the cheek and leg
it warms your soul and body and
it stills the tiny voice within
that warns in vain against your sin
and love in the tall tall grass

now August is a wicked month
it leaves the lost alone
a hand outstretched a fleeting smile
come hither now and stay awhile
and love will warm a lonely child
down here in the tall tall grass

now August is a wicked month
romances spring and die
when autumn comes the season turns
the pain of leaving starts to burn
reality we start to learn
from love in the tall tall grass

BIG BLUE BALLOON

I follow a big blue balloon
through the carnival spring afternoon
isn't it wild
to be lost like a child
chasing a big blue balloon

I follow a big blue balloon
through the carnival spring afternoon
at the end of the string
is a groovy young thing
pulling her big blue balloon

but wait just a moment I stop
and buy me a green lollipop
and talk to the man
with the canes in his hand
and the windup rabbits that hop

I follow a big blue balloon
through the carnival spring afternoon
just hoping she'll wait
when she gets to the gate
she'll be holding her big blue balloon

but wait just a moment I sigh
I think I must stop for a ride
I'm a sucker for clowns
and a merry go round
when it only will cost me a dime

then follow a big blue balloon
through the carnival late afternoon
and now I am running
don't worry I'm coming
hold on to your big blue balloon

MOUTH TO MOUTH RESUSCITATION

mouth to mouth
resuscitation
good for the country
good for the nation
nothin' quickens
your respiration
like a li'l ole bit
of that sweet sensation
that mouth to mouth
resuscitation

I dreamt last night
that Brigitte Bardot
was drownin' in the clutches
of a big undertow
and guess who the life guard
her only salvation
with that mouth to mouth
resuscitation

we'll do it every day
don't do it annual
on page fifteen
of your first aid manual
and through the whole book
their wildest creation's
that mouth to mouth
resuscitation

fat folks do it
skinny folks do it
Elizabeth Taylor
and Richard Burton do it
and even the French
got their own stylization
of that mouth to mouth
resuscitation

TOBACCO

tobacco is
an Indian weed
and from the ground
it do proceed
roll it
chew it
sniff it
smoke it
in your corncob pipe
you stoke it
comes in tin
or box
or pack
or you can buy it
by the sack . . .
filtered, strained
or mentholated
burley, twist
or airiated
tee
oh
bee
a
see see oh
yeah
that's the stuff for me
(short banjo interlude)
smoke tobacco
Indian weed
as from your lungs
the smoke proceeds
People smoke from
Main to Greenville

Hackensack to Bakersfield . . .
people smoke from
Nome to Dorset
TV doctors do endorse it
(or they did when I
wrote this song)
But beware the
bear named Smokey . . .
douse that butt
or Wheeling Stogey
tee oh be a see see oh
yeah, that's the stuff
for me
NOW . . . smoke tobacco
Indian weed
as from your nose the smoke
proceeds
the surgeon general
says you're doomed . . .
sitting in his
smoke filled room . . .
those that smoke
and think it's
sporty
may drop dead
before they're forty . . .
as I sit back and
puff on mine
this wicked
national pastime
tee oh bee a
see see oh
yeah
kill me dead
someday . . .

I DIDN'T KNOW THE WORLD WOULD LAST THIS LONG

I stumble through a yellow field
of dying grass
in front of me some happy people
quickly pass
inhaling deep the air
while love goes flying high
while younger hands in distant windows
wave goodbye

I forgot to live
in oh so many ways
I though I saw the numbers
marked on all the days
I trembled at the warnings
of the sad old men
beware my son the earth
is coming to an end

but now a breeze of simple truth
blows through my hair
striking down the fences
in my vacant stare
I'm stretching out my arms to fly
I know I'm free
I find I'm getting younger now
the more I see

I didn't know the world
would last this long
I didn't know I'd ever
sing this song
I didn't know how right
I could be wrong
and I didn't know the world
would last this long

words of fear go spinning out
across the land
to those who need the guidance
of a reassuring hand
while someone softly singing now
comes walking by
suddenly they'll find their voice
and then they'll cry

I didn't know the world
would last this long
I didn't know I'd ever
sing this song
I didn't know how right
I could be wrong
and I didn't know the world
would last this long

CALIFORNIA EARTHQUAKE

oh they tell me they've exploded
the underground blast
and what they say is happening's
gonna happen at last
that's the way it appears
and they tell me the fault line
runs right through here

if that may be
then that may be
what's gonna happen's
gonna happen to me
that's the way it appears
and they tell me the fault line
runs right through here

Atlantis will rise
Sunset Boulevard will fall
and where the beach used to be
won't be nothing at all
that's the way it appears
and they tell me the fault line
runs right through here

mother nature's got gas
her diet's gone stale
see her acid indigestion
on the richter scale
that's the way it appears
and they tell me the fault line
runs right through here

MR JACKSON'S GOT NOTHING TO DO

now he lays on his bed
in his undershirt suit
with his newspaper tie
and his foam rubber boots
with his book of girly pictures
he is searching for the truth
Mr. Jackson's got nothing to do

now he sits in the swing
while the street turns blue
and nods at the policeman
doin' it too
and yawns when the world
come gallopin' through
Mr. Jackson's got nothing to do

now I pass by his door
and I look in his room
it's half past three
and it's the last week in June
the linoleum's bare
except for his shoes
Mr. Jackson's got nothing to do

remember Mr. Jackson
I know that you do
with his gold plated lighter
that was just like new
and Saturday night
he wore his wing tip shoes
Mr. Jackson's got nothing to do

RAILROAD STREET

the latchstring's in on your bedroom door
so you can't see who you've missed
champagne goin' to the critics
a bathtowel on your hips
rhinestones shinin' in your bridgework
flashin' in the floodlight's glare
mail order patent leather dancin' boots
Vitalis in your hair
you're too much and I can't take it
I'm sorry but I think I'll leave
back to see an old drunk I know
livin' on Railroad Street

with your profile turned to the sunset
and your image strapped in place
you memorize your adlibs
while you practice with your face
whet rock chin pointin' skyward
half shut eyes to the wind
your part time unemployed talent scouts
tell me you're the livin' end
you're a legend let's face it
I'm sorry but I've got to leave
gonna hock my soul to the laundromat
down on Railroad Street

you've rubbed off every subtle hint
of what you used to be
it's all right there in the eight by ten
with the headline plain to see
you're handing out your goblets full
of California wine
to hold aloft in noisy prayer

to the trophy on your shrine
you're too much and I can't hack it
I think I'd better leave
and see some man about a dog
down on Railroad Street

I didn't recognize you
till you autographed my cast
and someone whispered could that be
the Davidson County flash
I know you'd be unhappy if
you couldn't be a star
but I wonder if they realize
just who you really are
I know but I won't tell 'em
instead I think I'll leave
back to see your next of kin
livin' on Railroad Street

MAN SMOKING A CIGAR

how fatly you smoke your cigar
you're holding the world in a jar
your jowls are deflating
the smoke you're inhaling
as wisely you smoke your cigar

steadfastly behind your cigar
you lead all your troops into war
confusing the hometeam
by leaving a smoke screen
I salute when I see your cigar

big feet on the desk as you groan
to some other wheel on the phone
like kids with their playthings
we save your cigar rings
that you have tossed down from your throne

you wave your cigar in the air
controlling big things from your chair
while sideways you tell us
the things you can sell us
and draw a diagram there

without your cigar you are weak
it lies in the ashtray asleep
it's part of your makeup
you hope it will shake up
the boys that sit down at your feet

how greatly you chomp your cigar
while pulling the strings from afar
could it be maybe you just had a baby
three cheers as you smoke your cigar

HOW COME YOU BEIN SO GOOD TO ME?

you scratch my back
and wash my socks
you answer the door
when the preacher knocks
you scrub the floor
and fill my belly
with peanut butter
and apple jelly
you change the kid
at half past three
how come you bein'
so good to me

how come you come
each time I call
when I get hung up
in the hall
how come you come
each time I yell
from down inside
my lazy spell
how come you come
each time I scream
how come you bein'
so good to me

every time
the roof caves in
like a tooth paste ad
you sit and grin

and if you're mad
it sure don't show
when I announce
I gotta go
you fill my pipe
before I leave
how come you bein'
so good to me

how come you come
each time I groan
and carry me home
when I get stoned
how come you move
when I say go
how come you hop
when I say toad
how come you cook
when I say eat
how come you bein'
so good to me

you cut the wood
and slop the hogs
and dig post holes
and feed the dogs
patch up holes
in your cotton sack
drive the truck
to town and back
while I decorate your window
with my big rusty feet
how come you bein'
so good to me

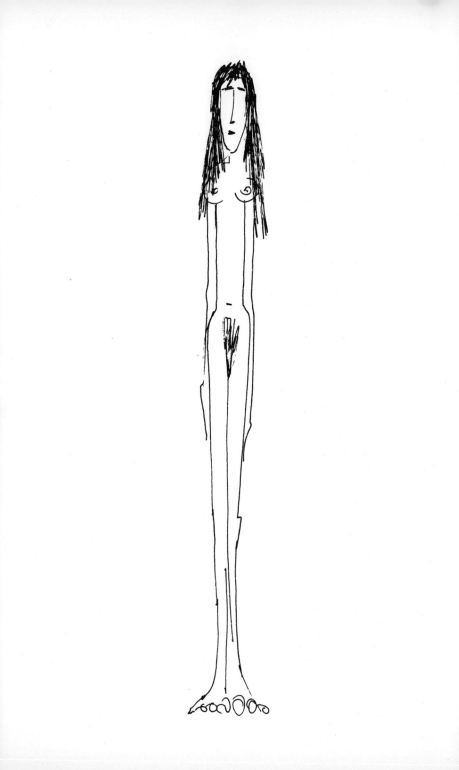

THE POOR OLD PRURIENT INTEREST BLUES

Napoleon is standing with
his pants upon the floor
there are naked painted people
in the poster on my door
Jack Lennon and his girlfriend
couldn't show me any more
won't someone please arouse
my prurient interest?

there's flesh throughout my magazines
it ripples pink and smooth
now the door fell off the bathroom
I can see what all you do
as I grab my flannel fig leaf
just to keep from being rude
have mercy on my poor old
prurient interest

won't you let me look myself
instead of waving it at me
don't leave it hanging out and sagging
over everything I see
don't take it off until I'm ready
let me have my little dreams
have mercy on my poor
old prurient interest

there's something back behind me
so I quickly turn around

the muffled sound of underwear
as it comes tumbling down
someone else is going natural
do I have to turn around?
have mercy on my poor old
prurient interest

It's TIME FOR ME TO GO

I've got creases cross my face
from watching you out of the
corner of my eye
I've got scratches on my heart
because you never look my way
when you come waltzing by
I've got goosebumps on my arms
from wantin' to fill up all that
dead air round your shoulders
and it's not because the heart's
turned down
or 'cause I've had too much
ice tea
or gettin' any colder

but I'm not supposed to know you
'cause there's someone else who watches
that I stay in line
and if I ever did step off
she'd probably pull out most her hair
and then start in on mine
so then I think it's best
I'd better leave it so
because I feel that gentle
tuggin' at my sleeve that means
it's time for me to go

WHY DO YOU DO ME LIKE YOU DO?

you hit me in the face
in the middle of the night
I try to sleep
while you want to fight
and it's just in your mind
that I didn't do right
why do you do me like you do

why do you do me like you do
have mercy on me
why do you do me like you do
when you know the only time
I ever ran around on you
was in your dreams

you better lay off all that coffee
'fore you climb into bed
or what ever's been giving you
that soap opera head
'cause one of these days
I'm gonna wake up dead
why do you do me like you do

now you've filled up my ears
and knocked me down on the floor
you've cut out my tongue
and left me tired and sore
and when I turn off the light
you think I'm asking for more
why do you do me like you do

LEFT HANDED WOMAN

left handed woman
you south pawed member
of the female gender
tender bender of my splendor
look at you
you do everything backward
from the way I do
you inside out
upside down
left handed woman you

left handed brown eyes
left handedly looking
left handedly holding
old right handed me
I tell you right
but it comes out left
and backward please woman
have mercy on me

THIS EVE OF PARTING

it's hard to think this eve of parting
turns to sand of summer gone
when both our minds are warped with parting
break the thought of nights alone

maybe I should turn in silence
tell myself I didn't care
curse the thought of your existence
loving every flaxen hair

flesh cries out don't move don't leave me
conscience runs till out of breath
sunrise pregnant with your leaving
creeping in like certain death

the pattern of the bird of love
that's wheeling on its dizzy way
tears me down to basic sorrow
useless for another day

it's hard to think this eve of parting
turns to sand of summer gone
when both our minds are warped with parting
break the thought of nights alone

flesh cries out don't move don't leave me
conscience runs till out of breath
sunrise pregnant with your leaving
creeping in like certain death

LOVE SONG IN 2/4 TIME

oh my
heart and soul
is hung up
in your magic spell
yes
even the way
you
put me down
'cause you
do it so well
but
if you
hate my guts
just half as much
as I love you
than I'd rather have
everyone else in the world
hate me
than for you to
do I
disappear
in front of
you when I sit down
and cry
when
all the rest of your
funky little friends
are
on your side
when you don't
notice me
ignoring you

that
puts me down
the warmness
of your coldness to me
spreads around
so if you
hate my guts
just half as much
as I love you
then
I'd rather have
everyone else in the world
hate me
than for you to

WHEN THE SKY BEGINS TO FALL

so you went and bought a book
and now you stand right here and say
you know it all
but where were you when
all the guns went off
the fire was hot
and
the sky began to fall
give an illustrated lecture
are you wantin' all the credit
are we all supposed to
stand around in awe
tell me where were you
when all the girls went home
and the sky began to fall

you are standin' right in front
of this old boy
you don't intend to even see
who could tell you some things
that most of which I do not think
that you'd believe
right now he's standin' there
a starin' holes into
the middle of your back
'cause he was really there
when you didn't even know
where it was at
better step aside
before he burns you
when the holes go clean on through the cloth
he knows you were a thousand miles away
back when the sky began to fall

he was standin' in the snow
and he didn't have a hat
or even shoes
with so much to load his mind
that he'd been happy
if it just had been the blues
I asked him what he thought
but he didn't have a chance to say a word
'cause before I finished up
you answered for him
with the fairy tale that
everybody here'd already heard
some impressions of some things you didn't see
but yet you think you might have saw
like you were leading in the stumble
and the rumble
when the sky began to fall

you're posin' for the camera
wonderin' what you haven't said
you ought to say
I wish they'd hurry up
and pin a ribbon on your chest
and maybe then you'd go away
all these battles that you fight
and all these mountains in the jungle
that you climb
you've produced in technicolor
on the movie lots a groanin'
in your mind
maybe next time that it happens
you would only come so far
then only look

and only when the smoke had cleared
then you could read about it
in some book
that's the safest way to learn
about the things you know
you hadn't really saw
and no one would see you
runnin' to your mother
when the sky begins to fall

JACK'S IN THE SACK

grandma screams
at the jersey cow
and talks about a girl
named fate
Alligator goes
on a drinkin' jag
and wipes his eyes
with hate
railroad steamboat
whistle too
Jim rehearses
yesterday's news
mom went to work
with the bathtub blues
and Jack's in the sack
with the grippe

Jack's in the sack
he's flat on his back
Jack's in the sack
with the grippe
Pete's in the street
with the nineteenth fleet
and Bob's got a girl
on the strip
Pete pulled the cork
and we all got stoned
the department of safety
took our phone
Mitch pulled the switch
and we all went home
and Jack's in the sack
with the grippe

out in the wildwood
sittin' on a chair
the sun goes down at night
tryin' to hog that center line
is a knock-down drag-out fight
Hubert Humphrey's got the flu
Cassius Clay and Timbuktoo
someone seized his biscuit too
and Jack's in the sack
with the grippe

put on your nightshirt
wear it in the hall
paint all the doorknobs black
build a fire with the TV Guide
put all your shoes in a sack
stick your hand in the same old grind
sing it to the tune of sweet Adeline
and sign your name
at the base of her spine
cause Jack's in the sack
with the grippe

Jack's in the sack
he's flat on his back
Jack's in the sack
with the grippe
I'm on the desk
with an army sword
George did a Cajun flip
Pete pulled the cork
and we all got stoned
sang about a place
where the buffalo roam
Mitch pulled the switch
and we all went home
and Jack's in the sack
with the grippe

WINDOWS

on these vacant streets of nightfall
try to fool myself I don't know where I'm goin'
in these gutters that I'm walkin'
the reflection of a thousand windows glowin'

some are laughin' some are cryin'
some are yawnin' as I quickly pass them by
something moving back behind I hear
a thumpin' or a sneeze sometimes a sigh

on those windows pretty windows
each contain their private dramas
I just pass outside just glancing up in vain
the flowers grow in boredom
and the curtains hang to mock me
is there not a chance that I might venture in

but the empty windows of your eyes
the shades are down to block my gaze within
your door is shut and boarded up
I stand in silence shivering in the rain
and the wind that bangs the garbage cans
just echoes insults deep within my tortured soul
it says move on you barefoot boy
there are no windows here for you
the minutes whisper time for you to go

on these windows pretty windows
fading back into their hallways
I just stand outside and watch them both in vain
the paint just peels in boredom
and the cobwebs hang to mock me
is there not a chance that I might venture in

CORN COB BLUES

the cowboy promoted
the wedding you know
between the songs
on his rock and roll show
the groom was thin
the bride was a tease
they courted to the sound
of his latest release
they both were members
of the back-up crew
the thin man a thinkin'
them corncob blues

the rain came down
and the crowd was slow
the cowboy hollered
and stubbed his toe
signs on trees
from here to town
hurricane Ethel
couldn't knock them down
the thin man stands
in waterlogged shoes
and keeps on a thinkin'
them corncob blues

the cowboy sweats
and walks the aisle
watchin' his money
in a sticky pile
he tears his napkin
there at the gate
he promoted the wedding

for two weeks straight
the thin man looks
while the law comes through
and keeps on a studyin'
them corncob blues

the bride sits there
and looks at the stars
a hound dog licks
his trusty guitar
the drummer tunes
to the key of g
the fiddle player
works for free
while scrapin' old popcorn
off his shoes
the thin man hums
them corncob blues

mama makes
the coffee boil
it's just as thick
as crankcase oil
the cowboy sends her
a kiss and a flower
he drinks ten cups
every quarter hour
the thin man wonders
if he's addin' booze
and whistles out loud
them corncob blues

brother got mad
at the skinny one
and the cowboy too
for all his fun
so brother talked
to the bride back stage
and he talked of love

in a white hot rage
the thin man wondered
if her love he'd lose
and he wrote another verse
to the corncob blues

the thin man smoked
and looked at his knees
and wondered if the crowd
would all be pleased
when the sun comes up
on another day
and he and the bride
were far away
he didn't think the cowboy'd
ever get through
so he could lose
them corncob blues

ANY MAN'S INFERNO

the vulture sits perched
on the bones of the dead
the sky and the earth
are smoldering red
the tree that drank life
from the chest of the soil
clutches in vain
to a limp pool of oil
the midgets are running
their horns are on fire
the women are screaming
and clutching the wire
that tears at the flesh
of the hands of the rich
who plead with the guard
for relief from the itch
but in heaven
they are not itching

their front teeth are ground
with the stone of a lie
spit blood on the hands
of those who ask why
a wheeze from a throat
that is scorched till it's black
from tendons that break
on the hooks of the rack
the four million faces
that keep moving on
the soles of their feet
are worn to the bone
the skins of the thirsty
hang limp from dead trees

and no ear is turned
to the rasp of their pleas
but in heaven
they are not thirsty

bodies are piled
in the pits of the damned
gasping for air
as they're buried in sand
a thick blistered tongue
licks out at a tear
that oozes in vain
from an eye filled with fear
the dogs are eating
that flesh that is torn
from the face of the nameless
forgot to be born
and pull out their fingernails
swing by their hair
naked and scorched
in the thick sulphur air
but in heaven
they are not suffering

over the river
of death no return
from then thru eternity
bodies will burn
the oars of the ferry
are out of their locks
the worms and the roaches
crawl over the rocks
the ants and the locusts
swarm down on the meat
that stinks on the bones
that outline defeat
the face of the clock
melts down in the pools

destroying all hope
for all of the fools
but there are no fools
in heaven

No

NO
absolutely not
never
my negative answer
NO possible
remote chance
that there could
ever be the
faintest glimmer of
optimism on the subject
NO, I will not
carry your gunnysack
NO, I will not
loan you ten dollars
NO, you cannot have
half of my popsicle
NO, I don't care if
you ever come back
NO what I mean?
NOtary public
NOtary sojack
NO more
NO less
NO smoking
NO parking
NO soap
NO littering
NO loitering
NO drinking
on the dance floor
NO minors allowed
NO rest stops
between here and

Wichita
NO chrome on the
lesser priced models
NO money down
NO body
NO thing
NO end
NO beginning
NO middle
NO top
NO bottom
NO inside
NO emptiness
everybody
NOs
and you should
NO that the
next time you want to
NO the answer will
still be
NO

I SHOULDA WORE MY BIRTHDAY SUIT

you took my watch
you took my chain
you took my sunshine
and my rain
you took my food
you took my drink
you even took
the kitchen sink

yeah I think
I shoulda wore my
birthday suit
no kinda socks
and one old boot
and left behind
my Stetson hat
so I wouldn't feel the cold
on my way back
you're too slick
Mrs. Rooty Toot Toot
I shoulda wore
my birthday suit

you took my sody
'fore I'se through
yeah and took
the car keys too
didn't you leave me
any fun
would you believe
my chewin' gum

you got my watch
and all my time
then skinned me outa my
very last dime
if this is what they call
destitute
then I shoulda showed up
in my birthday suit

THE DIRTY OLD AIR THAT HANGS OVER OUR TOWN

up the short stairway
and to the first floor
press on the buttons
and wait for the car
hear the bell jingle
and know that it's stopped
crowd on the elevator
and ride to the top

then it's up in the clouds
halfway up to the moon
to stand at the edge
of a glass enclosed room
pretend I'm a bird
that's just flying around
in the dirty old air
that hangs over our town

it's down in the alley
then out on the street
where the warm summer breeze
smells like old rotten meat
a flower is blooming
a pale shade of gray
but what do I care
it's a beautiful day

I'm feeling a sunbeam
I think over there
but I can't really tell
'cause it's up in the air
that hangs around useless
for anyone now
it's too thick to breathe
and it's too thick to plow

then it's up in the clouds
halfway up to the moon
to stand at the edge
of a glass enclosed room
pretend I'm a bird
that's just flying around
in the dirty old air
that hangs over our town

SPRINGTIME ALL OVER AGAIN

I do pushups with my heart
to see this railroad station picture
that I've found
and this two dimension smile of yours
that mocks me tho it never makes a sound
still I'm watching all the drugstores
and the laundrys and the newsstands
but you hardly ever seem
to come around

in winter empty rooms I've laid
awake to crumple up my dirty sheet
rehearsing till I'm sorry
all the things that I might say
if we should meet
if it be way down on Broadway
or maybe on Division
or over by the City Hall
or if by chance it be
on Commerce Street

and the steam pipes rattle
and the cold winds blow
through radiator visions
of ice and snow
I think I see you quickly go
and it's springtime
all over again

I give a dime for coffee
and a dollar
for some steamy greasy plate

I peel my jacket from my back
and hang it there to drip
upon the grate
I think you might have
been here yes
but if you have
you've melted
or you weren't
or I was just
a little late

I'VE HEARD THAT TEARSTAINED MONOLOGUE YOU DO THERE BY THE DOOR BEFORE YOU GO!

sometimes I get to thinkin'
that I've passed this point in life
one time before
like the rerun of some movie
that I saw a thousand Saturdays ago

and I get the feeling
that I know
exactly what you're gonna do
and say before it happens
in each scene

I find myself rehearsing
for that blackout situation
when the punchline reaches out
and punches me

I always play
the same old part
the good guy gets the girl
I wind up dead
those rides
into the sunset
when the credits
start to roll
are only flashed upon

the screen
inside my head

the show is done
the lights go up
I throw my empty
popcorn box away
go back to unreality
on rubber legs I walk
into the day

but life is never logical
the faces change
the lines all stay the same
I know the cues where I come in
the exits but
I can't recall your name

so save your breath
don't tell me how
it all comes out
somehow I think I know
I've heard that
tearstained monologue
you do there by the door
before you go

what makes me take you
by the hand
and stand around in line
one time again
and see the same old madness
while I ask
is this the place
where I came in

so save your breath
don't tell me how

it all comes out
somehow I think I know
I've heard that
tearstained monologue
you do there by the door
before you go

EMPTY AFTERNOON OF SUMMER LONGING

as I look at you I wonder
what would happen if I brushed away
the curtains of your hair
and quickly kissed you
and stumbling for some words to say
my mind goes spinning on its way
with images of future days
to miss you

and the sun is easing down
as it grows later
and soon I know you'll rise
and say farewell
and here we are imprisoned
in the empty afternoon
of summer longing

across this coffee cup I see
a face now cloaked in mystery
while pondering this peace
that could be violence
the night is fast approaching
in its emptiness surrounding us
I'm pressed to make a move
or turn in silence

you slowly smile across at me
I wonder if you're free to be
in love am I too blind to see
while hungry
for when you're resting by my side
in nothing but the night to hide

the lips that say I'm satisfied
it's worth it

an hour becomes the flickering
of an eyelash
an undecided moment
out of sight
and here we are imprisoned
in the empty afternoon
of summer longing

you may be many miles away
just living out some broken day
while just a picture of you
stays and dances
the shadows streak the plaster wall
I'm nervous as I sit and stall
and wonder should I reach
and take my chances

and night comes sneaking up
on simple daydreams
I'll curse myself
before the morning breaks
yet here we are imprisoned
in the empty afternoon
of summer longing

THE SIX O'CLOCK TRAIN AND A GIRL WITH GREEN EYES

it's hard to concentrate on waiting
wondering if she will know my face
and trying to remember
if it might have been the time
or maybe might have been the place

in an underground railroad station
just out of the rain
so much depends on the six o'clock train
and a girl with green eyes

the hands of the subway clock
are almost straight up and down
and way back in that dark black tunnel
I thought I heard a sound
will she know me when she sees me
or wait to hear my voice
when I see her walkin' through the steam
in the maddening rush hour noise

so silly in my nervousness
so crazy in my fear
I asked a man with a brown suit on
does the six o'clock stop here
re reassured me quickly
and turned as if in pain
and I wondered maybe he like I
depended on the train

in an underground railroad station
just out of the rain
so much depends on the six o'clock train
and a girl with green eyes

GO HOME GIRL

you might wake up some cold morning
there won't be no chocolate Easter eggs
to hunt for
no more roaches in the ashtray
no more levis hangin'
on the bathroom door
just a trail of empty coffee cups
too bad there isn't some one there
to see them

go home girl
and find somebody else
you can depend on

to the rafters and the ceilings
there's a rise of liquid sound
the hour suffers
and you're underneath your duster
painting circles on the floor
where you were crying
go buy yourself a taxi cab
and live in front of
Saks Fifth Avenue window
go home girl
and find somebody else
you can depend on

go home and find your cameos
go home and try and find
your aging mother
go home and set the table
and be there to hold her hand
as she gets older

go home and read your magazines
I'll see you when the streets
return to silver
go home girl
and find somebody else
you can depend on

LIKE UNTO A MOCKINGBIRD

all around somebody else's pad
you stumble as you chase the latest fad
if you're confused with all the things you find
just wait until the crowd makes up your mind

comin' back repeating every word
repeating all the things you overheard
the band wangon rumble past I sit here on the curb
like an echo
you are like unto a mockingbird

as long as you can sing their style of song
you won't be lonely you can tag along
pasted on your face a sickly grin
hopin' that someone will say you

dark eyes shiftin' round take in a lot
notin' who is here and then who's not
careful that you keep your standin' clean
away from those with whom you can't be seen

comin' back repeating every word
repeating all the things you overheard
the band wagons rumble past I sit here on the curb
like an echo
you are like unto a mockingbird

here lately you don't speak or even look
because my name's not written in their book
but if they turn my different ways to see
you'd be the first to proudly stand by me

MINUS THE WOMAN

I'm minus the woman
a love that's withdrawn
badly bent over backwards
with the thought of her gone

her closet is empty
the dresser is bare
except for the cobwebs
laced up on the mirror
the wallpaper peels and
hangs down to the floor
too tired to stick
to the boards anymore
no tick tock the silence
the hands of the clock
are frozen so stiffly
the sound is in shock
I should go and set it
and wind it alone
but she's got the turnkey
and now she is gone
sometimes when I'm tired
of ignoring the gloom
I think I'm bein' studied
by the walls of the room
and when I'm not watchin'
too misty to see
these four walls start to creepin'
real slowly towards me

I'm minus the woman
a love that's withdrawn
badly bent over backwards
with the thought of her gone

110

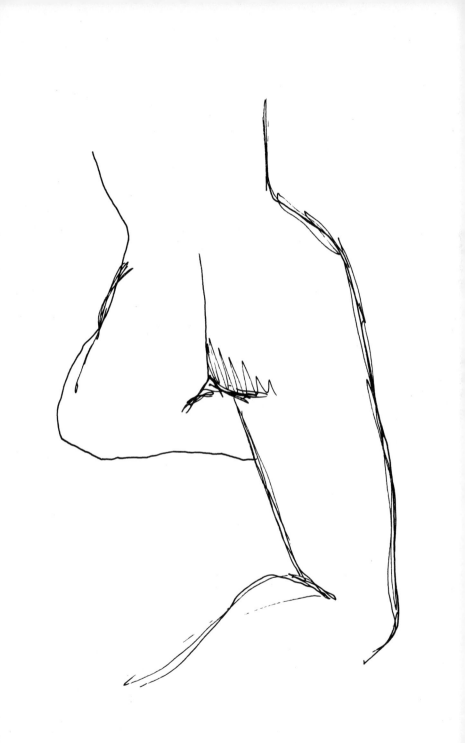

I RECKON

who is this demon
they call commercial
whose eyes blank and little bells ring
as it gathers in the pot
and then stares
balefully
at its audience of
struggling young artists
who are all thinkin'
comersh . . . cmere
I reckon

who is this demon
called commercial
walkin' in the shiny black grooves
molding classifying and
restricting
those
who are already restricted
and
caged inside a melody
I reckon

had I not made this record
I would have still
made these songs
and sung them to my family
my friends
and then
softly to myself
I reckon

these are
some of the things
that have drifted by my eyes
seeped into my ears
and now have passed from my mouth
and may the demon have mercy
I reckon

ORPHAN OF WORLD WAR TWO

I'm just an orphan of world war two
a parent of world war three
if I choose to lay down
with the builders of bombs
and the vendors of insanity

and still go along
with it all right or wrong
if it's something I somehow can't buy

I'm just an orphan of world war two
rehearsing for world war three
beaten up in Chicagos streets
for the cameras of N B C

the freedom I had
you have labeled a fad
to be cured with scissors and soap

I'm just an orphan of world war two
I've laid down in front of your place
I've pleaded and sung at the top of my lungs
but I'm something you don't want to face

just kick me around
in the suburbs of town
till I drop out and split for the north

I'm just an orphan of world war two
a parent of world war three
if I choose to lay down
with the builders of bombs
and the vendors of insanity

THE
WART

in my heart
there's a tender spot
of a magic sort
for the wart the wart
the little fat wart
stomp your foot
and give a little snort
for the wart

well the buyer of the chicken sticks
the husband of the mother
and the mother is the changer
and the feed and the washer
and the father is the holder
of the wart the wart
the little fat wart
stomp your foot
and give a little snort
for the wart

well wart father wart mother
wart sister wart brother
grandfather grandmother
this 'n that 'n somethin' other
just wart people grinnin' at the
wart the wart
the little fat wart
stomp your foot
and give a little snort
for the wart

EVE OF MY MULTIPLICATION

on the eve of my multiplication
I tried to look back
to an eve not twenty-six years ago
and I saw another man
on the eve of his multiplication
and I wondered if he looked back
because early the next morning
there I was
and early tomorrow morning
there you'll be
and some day
you'll look back
on days filled with sunshine
and days filled with sorrow
and days filled with love
and sometimes you'll wonder
if there'll be a tomorrow
and you'll see books and toys
and odd jobs
and other little girls and boys
and sometimes you'll hate me
and sometimes you'll love
then someday you'll love
as I have
and before you realize it
as your father
and my father
and his father
and his father
before him
realized
that you
on the eve
of your multiplication

THE GOOD OLD ELECTRIC WASHING MACHINE CIRCA . 1943

well
I
sure do miss
that
good old
electric washing machine
the one that
we ain't got round here
no more and
I sure do miss that
big round tub
and them
stompin' swinging sounds
and I
miss them groovy puddles
on the floor
'cause the new one just goes
hmmmmmmmmmmmmmmmmmmm
but the old one went
(demonstrate throat warp)
well . . .
I cry when I see
that brand new
automatic washing machine
'cause
I'm sentimental
for the old machine
still yet
'cause the old one

really looked like a
real live washing machine
but the new one
just looks more like a
television set . . .
and the new one just
sits there and goes
hmmmmmmmmmmmmmmmmmmmm
mmmmmmmmmmmmmmmmmmmm
mmmmmmmmmmmmmmmmmmmm
but the old one goes
(demonstrate throat warp)

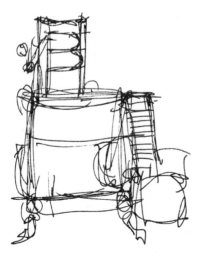

WHO'S THAT?

who's that
hidin' in the tree trunks
who's that
standin' there afar
who's that
hidin' 'neath the back porch
who's that
underneath the car
who's that
creepin' by the window
who's that
walkin' on the roof
who's that
peckin' on the bedroom wall
I don't know do you?

who's that
runnin' by the mailbox
who's that
lettin' out that groan
who's that
slidin' down the drain pipe
who's that
talkin' on the phone
who's that
leavin' them bathtub rings
who drank my mountain dew
who's that
talkin' on the radio
I don't know do you?

who's that
stinkin' up the schoolhouse
who's that
gettin' all the praise
who's that
stole my fountain pen
who ate my mayonnaise
who's that
hangin' round the drugstore
who's that
used my glue
who's that
makin' all the money
I don't know do you?

THE SAILBOAT SONG

faint pictures of my childhood
lie floundering in your wake
that worries of tomorrow at your bow
your spinnaker a white balloon
your mainsail proud and tall
to me you are the very soul of now

I'm dizzy on your teakwood deck
my arms around your mast
insane inside your cabin soft and warm
then drifting off to sleep
your fingers loose along my face
in contented disbelief of early morn

to me you are the moment
the present breath of life as
together we are slicing through the spray
the second buried deep
within the mystery of your love
not shades of things to come
or yesterday

faint pictures of my childhood
lie floundering in your wake
the worries of tomorrow at your bow
your spinnaker a white balloon
your mainsail proud and tall
to me you are the very soul of now

MY FACE

my face I don't mind it
I'm standing behind it
it hangs down in front
by my hair
it studies the cards
all the aces and spades
but it don't have to call
which they aire
I've taught it to smile
and to wrinkle its nose
and to froth at the mouth
when it's mad
I've taught it to yawn
and to laugh and to snarl
and to hang out its lip
when it's sad

my face I don't mind it
I live here behind it
quite tightly it's wedged
'tween my ears
it acts like a wall
over which lies the world
so they can't read my hopes
and my fears
in front of my chin
pass the sights and the smells
and the songs and the sound
of the horn
of the traffic and blarin'
and honkin' and screechin'
of time since the day
I was born

my face if you find it
I'm back here behind it
it's only a mask
for the soul
it don't have no lines
you can follow as such
for it's only a part
not the whole
while you could be talkin'
or snarlin' or coughin'
or holdin' your head
while you weep
in back of this face
I could watch or be singin'
or sometimes I might
be asleep

IN LIKE OF

like you yes
and moreover well
more intense than
just sit down a spell
gets harder to
whisper goodbye
I sigh
and see
for me
that it's true
that I'm so deep
in like
that I'm almost
in love
with you

like you yes
and very much so
it's weird but
that's how it goes
gets harder to
whisper so long
how wrong
I would be
to think
it's not true
that I'm so deep
in like
that I'm almost
in love
with you

like is a word
a verbal abstraction
for how much subtraction
from love must you make
to be back in like of
whoever it was that
you were in love of at first
I don't know
nor do you

like you yes
I cannot deny
and in spite of
the things that I try
gets harder to
whisper farewell
so tell
me to stay
I just may
cause its true
that I'm so deep
in like
that I'm almost
in love
with you

THE LITTLE OLD LONESOME LITTLE OLD CIRCLE SONG

just a lonesome little circle
with a lonesome little arrow
extending from my lonesome
little side

just a lonesome little circle
with its nothing all around me
it's so lonesome
that I sit alone
and cry

another little circle
a pretty little circle
it doesn't seem to care
that much for me

a pretty little ring
around the rosy
little circle
with a pretty little
plus sign underneath

it's hard to be a circle
a lonesome little circle
without that certain circle
next to me

she's gone and left me blue
little circle
number two
with a pretty little
plus sign underneath

so I'm swimming all around
with my arrow hanging down
as glad as any circle
you might see

a lonesome little circle
how I miss that little circle
with a pretty little
plus sign underneath

NO END OF LOVE

I'd like to go where you go
and see the things you see
I like to hear the sounds you hear
and breathe the air you breathe
and hurt for you in times of pain
and smile when things are right again
and love you like there was no end of love
no end of love

with you I'd like to do the things
that I have done before
that have a different meaning now
that wasn't there before
as if I'd started out anew
just when I stumbled onto you
for now my dreams divide in two for you
no end of love

I'd like to sing the songs you sing
and play the games you play
I'd like to walk the roads you walk
and let you lead the way
I'd like to get the notes you send
and keep you dry from a summer's rain
and love you like there was no end of love
no end of love

GENTLE ON MY MIND

it's knowin' that
your door is always
open and your path
is free to walk
that makes me tend
to leave my sleeping bag
rolled up and stashed
behind my couch
and it's knowing I'm not
shackled by
forgotten words and bonds
and the inkstains
that have dried
upon some line
that keeps you in the
back roads
by the rivers of my memory
that keeps you ever gentle
on my mind

it's not clinging
to the rocks and ivy
planted on some column
now that binds me
or somethin' that
somebody said
because they thought
we fit together walkin' . . .
it's just knowin' that
the world will not be
cursing or forgiving
when I walk along
some railroad track

129

and find
that you're movin'
on the back roads
by the rivers of my memory
and for hours you're just gentle
on my mind

though the wheat fields
and the clothes lines
and the junkyards
and the highways come
between us
and some other woman cryin'
to her mother 'cause she
turned
and I was gone
I still might run in silence
tears of joy might stain my face
and a summer sun might
burn me till I'm blind
but
not to where I
cannot see you
walkin' on the back roads
by the rivers flowin' gentle
on my mind

I dip my cup of soup
back from the gurgling
crackling cauldron
in some train yard
my beard a rough'ning coal pile
and a dirty hat pulled low
across my face
through cupped hands
round a tin can
I pretend I hold you
to my breast and find

that you're wavin' from the back roads
by the rivers of my memory
ever smiling ever gentle
on my mind

CRYSTALLIA DAYDREAM

the words that cut my flesh
and the lash upon my brain is now forgotten
and the lead that hardens in my system
melts in sweet emotion turns to gold
and all the things now past are strangely worth it
my yesterdays are buried deep and cold

there's nothing now worth learning
and there's nothing I can look to I can think of
and there's nothing said or written
or recorded or remembered I should know
except the music of your pale voice singing
that loosens up the muscles of my soul

right now I'd give the world
that hangs around me like a circus
to know I'd never rise or walk or stand
and this could last forever and a weekend
and I'd die of happiness beneath your hand

the sun is smiling out
on miles of emptiness in all directions
the light caress of yellow hair
I'm flat upon my belly in the sand
and my skin is marching off in endless drumbeats
as you trace its empty canyons with your hand

the hours go flashing by
like the blinking of an eyelid
and the insults and the sorrow
of the day before are dead and gone for good
and tomorrow is a promise somehow pending
when everything unsaid is understood

right now I'd give the world
that hangs around me like a circus
to know I'd never rise or walk or stand
and this could last forever and a weekend
and I'd die of happiness beneath your hand

THE GIRL WITH THE LONG BROWN HAIR

I'm in love with the girl
with the long brown hair
that grows and entwines
and encircles me there
in my captive space
a slave to her love
as it brushes my face
where it hangs from above
I could sit and eat ice cream
the day long
and stare
at the beautiful girl
with the long brown hair

and it weaves in my fingers
comes up
'tween my ties
like mahogany silk
wherever it goes
and it trails through my oatmeal
then flies down the hall
in long stringy shadows
that flicker the wall
till I'm high as a seagull
just coasting on air
I'm in love with the girl
with the long brown hair

I'm in love with the girl
with the long brown locks
and I hope that she never tries
dye or peroxide
or scissors or curlers
or something like that
where she has to parade
in some weird looking hat
just grow it for miles
let it blow in the air
I'm in love with the girl
with the long brown hair

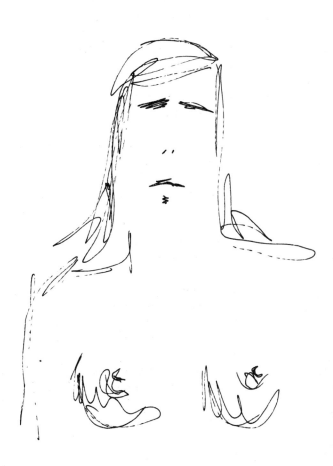

I'M STILL HERE

trains are runnin' towards each other
shotguns are pointed at my head
tornado clouds are formin' o'er the crossroads
h bombs a fallin' towards my bed
but I'm still here
I'm still here . . . now how 'bout that
my city may be fallin'
but I'm still here

the assassination squad has got their orders
the repossession man is on his way
the landlady's given me her notice
I'll get pitched out with the trash just any day
but I'm still here
I'm still here . . . now ain't that slick
I may have lost my lunch box
but I'm still here

the moths have ate my shirts and all my britches
I never had a hat so I don't care
I haven't had a meal since the fire went out
and all you do is stand around and stare
but I'm still here
I'm still here . . . and still breathin'
I might not see you laughin'
but I'm still here

my cigarettes are gone and so's my money
so are all my nerves and all my teeth
my hair is fallin' out I'm gettin skinny
my friends are either dead or on relief
but I'm still here
I'm still here . . . so don't sweat it
I might be good as buried
but I'm still here

BEFORE THEY TOW MY CAR AWAY

today I felt the cruel world
through the skin of your rose colored touch
and an hour was better than nothing at all
in the knowing that that wasn't much

I'd like to eat your pretzels my love
I'd like to stay all day but I must
kiss you quick and run my love
before they tow my car away

you haven't got change for a dollar
besides it won't work after four
as soon as I lace up my work shoes
I think I should head for the door

I'd like to drink your coffee my love
I'd like to stay all day but I must
kiss you quick and run my love
before they tow my car away

SHINY RAILS OF STEEL

in the dirty basements of my brain
the odor of the iron train
as steam rise up in opaque cloud
and silence breaks like glass
beneath the whistle clear and loud
and tie rods clank like robots
as machinery slowly moves
to make its effort
down these shiny rails of steel

and through some window passing now
I think I see her looking out
her nose pressed round upon the glass
that flickers like a piece of jade
as it goes flashing past
in dirty Pullman coaches
sliding out to meet the dawn
beside the stockyards
on these shiny rails of steel

so I turn myself around
and walk along the wet concrete
that seems to crack beneath my burden
and the years of boiler heat
around the mail trucks and the baggage
as I drag my shoes and go
to find a dismal bench somewhere
within the depot's yellow glow
away from salad dripping kitchens
from the seams of dining cars
that lay like diamonds
on these shiny rails of steel

138

through the speakers of my memory
I can hear the sad refrain
call the number of the loading gate
to catch the southbound train
her suitcase like a coffin
in the creases of my hand
then suddenly I'm all alone
with no place else to stand
as cars all chunk together
and the steps are moved away
and then she's gone
upon these shiny rails of steel

I WON'T KNOW WHY I WENT TILL AFTER I GET BACK, MAYBE

well I think
I gotta go somewhere
but I don't rightly know
just when
I'm not even sure
what's gonna go down
or if I'm comin' back again
and I may not do
much of anything
and we both
know where that's at
'cause I won't know why
I even go
till after I
get back

sometimes the hardest
thing you can do
is just get up and
walk on out
when leavin's the only
thing on your mind
for which you have
no doubt
instinct babe
for all it's worth
can only tell me that
so how can you expect me

to know why I went
till after I
get back

I just might go
anywhere
I don't care
I don't care
if there's anything there
I'll find it

well I didn't know
you would be someplace
till I saw you there
myself
when I didn't even know
you'd be anywhere at all
or that I'd be
anywhere else
every other reason
I've had for leavin'
is gone
and I'm sure of that
'cause I don't know why
I even go
till after I
get back

one last word
of caution
everything
in this book
(including the cover)
has been printed
upside down
with the
exception of the
last word
of this
poem.